Fact Finders®

ADVENTURES ON THE AMERICAN FRONTIER

STRIKE IT RICH!

THE STORY OF THE CALIFORNIA GOLD RUSH

BY BRIANNA HALL

Consultant:
Greg Voelm
President
Sacramento County Historical Society
Sacramento, California

CAPSTONE PRESS
a capstone imprint

Fact Finders are published by Capstone Press,
1710 Roe Crest Drive, North Mankato, Minnesota 56003
www.capstonepub.com

LIBRARY OF CONGRESS CATALOGING-IN-PUBLICATION DATA

Hall, Brianna.

Strike it rich! : the story of the California Gold Rush / by Brianna Hall.

pages cm.—(Fact finders: Adventures on the American frontier)

Summary: "Explores the California Gold Rush by examining the causes leading up to it and the immediate and lasting effects it had on the people and places involved"—Provided by publisher.

Includes bibliographical references and index.

ISBN 978-1-4914-0184-2 (library binding); ISBN 978-1-4914-0189-7 (paperback);

ISBN 978-1-4914-0193-4 (ebook PDF)

1. California—Gold discoveries—Juvenile literature. 2. California—History—1846–1850—Juvenile literature. 3. Frontier and pioneer life—California—Juvenile literature. I. Title.

F865.H165 2014

979.4'04—dc23   2014007815

EDITORIAL CREDITS

Jennifer Huston, editor; Sarah Bennett, series designer; Kazuko Collins, layout artist; Wanda Winch, media researcher; Tori Abraham, production specialist

PHOTO CREDITS

Art Resource, N.Y.: The Art Archives, 5; The Bridgeman Art Library: © Look and Learn/Private Collection/Roger Payne, 4; The California Historical Society, (CHS2009.138), 16; Capstone, 17; Corbis: Yogi, Inc., 9; Courtesy Levi Strauss & Co. Archives, 29; Courtesy Scotts Bluff National Monument: William Henry Jackson, 8; Getty Images: George Eastman House, 19, Underwood Archives, 18; Hanging Out ©Heide Presse, 21; Library of Congress: Prints and Photographs Division, 6, 26, 28; North Wind Picture Archives, 12, 15, 22; Shutterstock: 06photo, book page background, Don Bendickson, 10, Gary Saxe, 24, homy design, leather design, Itana, sunburst design, ixer, 1 (banner), LongQuattro, 7, 17 (compass), Luca Moi, 25, Miloje, 25 (top right), optimarc, 20, Picsfive, grunge paper design; SuperStock: Huntington Library, cover; Zazzle, 11

PRIMARY SOURCE BIBLIOGRAPHY

Page 11—Revere, Joseph Warren. *A Tour of Duty in California.* New York: C. S. Francis & Co., 1849.

Page 11—Stillson, Richard T. *Spreading the Word: A History of Information in the California Gold Rush.* Lincoln, Neb.: University of Nebraska Press, 2006.

Page 21—Schlissel, Lillian. *Women's Diaries of the Westward Journey.* New York: Schocken Books, 2004.

Page 23—Shufelt, S. *A Letter from a Gold Miner.* San Marino, Calif.: Friends of the Huntington Library, 1944.

Page 23—Van Dyke, Walter. "Early Days in Klamath." *Overland Monthly*, Vol. XVII, No. 104, August 1891.

Page 27—"The Gold Rush." *American Experience.* Directed by Randall MacLowry. 2006. www.pbs.org/wgbh/amex/goldrush/filmmore/pt.html

Page 28—Sutter, John. "The Discovery of Gold in California." *Hutchings' California Magazine*, November 1857.

Printed in the United States of America in Stevens Point, Wisconsin.

032014   008092WZF14

TABLE OF CONTENTS

———— ◆ ————

CHAPTER 1

GOLD FEVER!

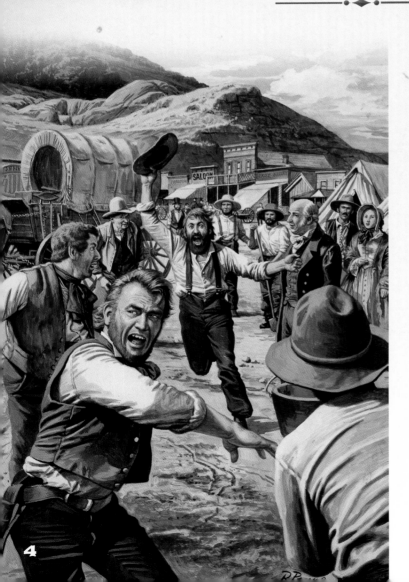

"Gold! Gold from the American River!" In May 1848, shopkeeper Sam Brannan ran through the streets of San Francisco, California, waving a bottle of gold nuggets above his head. San Francisco's residents had already read in the newspaper that gold had been discovered nearby, but no one believed it. Sam Brannan knew that seeing is believing.

Excitement was in the air after Sam Brannan spread the news that gold had been discovered near Sutter's Mill.

By 1849 the streets of San Francisco were nearly abandoned as residents left to mine for gold.

When Brannan brought his exciting news to San Francisco, nearly all of its 850 residents left to find gold. One account suggests that there were only women, children, and five men remaining. Farmers abandoned their crops. Shoemakers and bakers left their shops. Ships sat empty in San Francisco Bay when the crews took off to mine for gold. Even the local newspaper, the *California Star*, stopped printing the news on June 14, 1848, when the reporters left to seek their fortunes. From 1848 to 1854, around 300,000 people made their way to California. The gold rush was on!

Before California Was California

Wild and *lawless* describe northern California before the gold rush. It seemed that everyone had a gun or a knife on hand—just in case. Wild cattle roamed the hills. Grizzly bears lived in the mountains. There were no paved roads, just hunting trails and wagon tracks. The American Indians, Mexicans, and American settlers living there did not trust one another. Too often, disagreements ended in murder.

In 1846, land disputes between the United States and Mexico led to the Mexican War (1846–1848). The war officially ended when the two countries signed the Treaty of Guadalupe Hidalgo on February 2, 1848. The treaty gave the United States more than 500,000 square miles (1.3 million square kilometers) of land. This land included present-day California, Nevada, Utah, and parts of Arizona, Colorado, New Mexico, and Wyoming. The treaty also established the Rio Grande as the southern border of Texas. Just days before the treaty was signed, workers in California made a big discovery that would grab the world's attention.

TERRITORY ACQUIRED FROM MEXICO

With the Treaty of Guadalupe Hidalgo, the United States gained land that would become all or part of several states.

WYOMING

NEVADA

UTAH

CALIFORNIA

COLORADO

ARIZONA

NEW MEXICO

■ Treaty of Guadalupe Hidalgo

THE AGE OF GOLD

John Sutter lived an adventurer's life. He was a grocer from Switzerland who traveled the world before settling in California. In 1839 he started Sutter's Fort. It was located near where the Sacramento and American Rivers meet, in what is now the capital city of Sacramento. Everyone who lived there worked for Sutter.

James Marshall and his crew were preparing the land to build a sawmill when Marshall found gold pebbles near the river.

Sutter wanted to build a sawmill to cut logs into boards. He hired James Marshall and a group of men for the job. They chose a spot for the mill about 50 miles (80 km) away from Sutter's Fort (in present-day Coloma) and got to work.

On January 24, 1848, Marshall picked up a few gold pebbles from a pile of rocks by the river. He showed them to the workers. One account says they laughed and called him crazy for thinking it was gold. Another story tells how the only woman with the work crew proved that the gold was real. Jennie Wimmer was making soap with a chemical called lye. She put the gold pebbles into the lye, and they did not dissolve or break apart. Instead they became shiny. That meant they were real gold!

Marshall traveled to Sutter's Fort to tell his boss about the discovery. After seeing the handful of shiny gold pebbles, Sutter also tested them and agreed that they were real gold. Soon the entire settlement, including Sam Brannan, knew about the gold. They left their jobs at Sutter's Fort in hopes of finding their fortunes mining for gold.

REAL GOLD OR FOOL'S GOLD?

How did Jennie Wimmer know the difference between fool's gold and real gold? She knew some of the properties of real gold. Properties are features that distinguish elements from one another. One property of gold is that it is dense, or difficult to destroy. Lye burns skin, but it won't destroy the surface of gold.

Fool's gold is a mineral called iron pyrite. It is brassy and yellow in color, so it is often mistaken for real gold. But fool's gold breaks apart in lye. Because the gold was real, it passed Jennie's test!

These pebbles resemble the gold that James Marshall found in 1848.

Read All About It!

Americans found out about the discovery of gold in California through the newspapers. On March 15, 1848 *The Californian* first reported that gold had been found. San Francisco's *California Star* printed a huge story about the discovery on April 1. Californians soon had gold fever!

But the news took months to spread throughout the United States. In August 1848, a military leader named Colonel Richard Mason wrote a letter to President James Polk. Mason estimated that miners were finding a total of $30,000 to $50,000 worth of gold, or more, per day! (That would be more than $1 million today!) Mason sent along a small bottle of pure gold as proof. The letter made mining sound easy: "The laboring man wants nothing but his pick and shovel and tin pan ... [M]any frequently pick gold out of ... rocks with their knives." President Polk shared Mason's report with Congress on December 5, 1848.

Ads like this one attracted men eager to strike it rich in California.

Soon newspapers across the country reported the discovery of gold in California. Headlines boasted "piles of gold," "treasure streams," and "thousands of jobs." Newspapers on the East Coast advertised cheap boat fares to San Francisco.

"The great discovery of gold ... has thrown the American people into a state of the wildest excitement ... Gold can be ... scooped up in tin pans at the rate of a pound of the pure dust a scoop ... 'Ho! for California!' is the cry everywhere."

—*California Herald*, December 26, 1848

11

CHAPTER 3

"HO! FOR CALIFORNIA!"

Around the country people imagined California as a place where streams flowed with gold and the Pacific coast glittered in the sun. The promise of a quick fortune attracted many. Shopkeepers, craftsmen, and lawyers left in search of adventure. Struggling farmers left their homes and families, leaving behind thousands of women to run farms and businesses. Freed slaves also headed to California, hoping for a fresh start.

Sailing to California was a long, exhausting, and uncomfortable journey.

Those with gold fever felt there was no time to lose. Gold seekers could travel to California by land or by sea. Both routes were dangerous, and travelers had no idea if they would survive the journey.

In 1849 about half the travelers came by sea. New York City and New Orleans became hubs for gold hunters looking to set sail. The cheapest and longest route went around the southern tip of South America at Cape Horn and then back up the Pacific coast. The trip could take six months or more. Some boats crashed on the rocky shores. Passengers became seasick on the choppy seas as bitter winds and ice storms tossed the boats to and fro.

A quicker route went across the **Isthmus** of Panama, a strip of land connecting the Atlantic and Pacific Oceans. This route took about three months, but it was just as risky. Travelers sailed up the Chagres River then crossed the isthmus on mules or on foot. In the jungles of Central America, they often became ill with deadly diseases, such as **malaria** or **yellow fever**. Travelers often died from heatstroke or exhaustion. Those who survived waited for weeks for ships heading to California.

isthmus—a narrow strip of land that has water on both sides and connects two larger sections of land

malaria—a serious disease that people get from mosquito bites; malaria causes high fever, chills, and sometimes death

yellow fever—an illness that can cause high fever, chills, nausea, and kidney and liver failure; liver failure causes the skin to become yellow, giving the disease its name

On the Wagon Train

Those who traveled to California by land gathered in frontier towns, such as Chicago, St. Louis, and Kansas City. An estimated 30,000 people headed west on wagon trains in 1849. They were mostly men, but a handful of women and children prepared for the dangerous journey too.

Folks in wagon trains set out in spring so their animals would have enough grass to eat on the trip. The overland journey to California took about six months. Travelers were challenged to survive as they crossed prairies, deserts, and mountains. River crossings were especially deadly. Some people drowned, and some caught **pneumonia** after sleeping in their wet clothes. Others died from **cholera** after drinking contaminated water.

ᶜᵒ FUN FACT ᵒᵛ

Some store owners advertised an unusual ointment called "California gold grease." According to reports, those who rubbed it on their bodies could roll down a mountain, and gold would stick to them. When they got to the bottom, they'd be covered in gold ... and rich.

pneumonia—a serious disease that causes the lungs to become inflamed and filled with a thick fluid that makes breathing difficult

cholera—a dangerous disease that causes severe sickness and diarrhea; cholera is caused by contaminated food or water

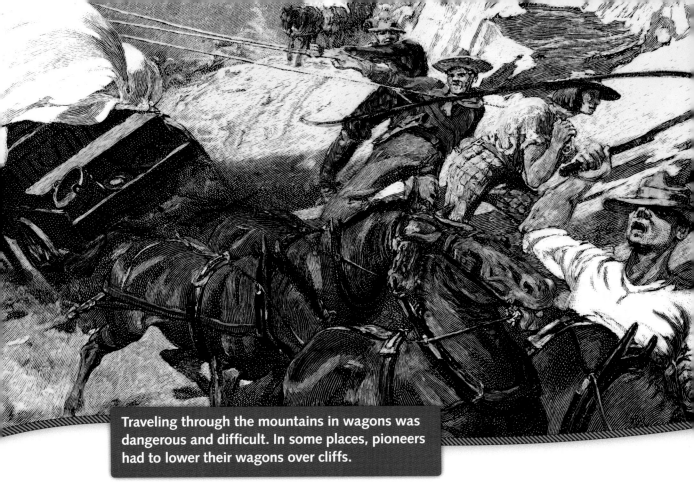

Traveling through the mountains in wagons was dangerous and difficult. In some places, pioneers had to lower their wagons over cliffs.

Some travelers took a shortcut through Utah's Great Salt Lake Desert, but it was even more difficult to navigate than the prairie. Travelers who lost their way died of thirst. Oxen, horses, and donkeys collapsed because there was no grass to eat. Finally, the Sierra Nevada mountains surprised travelers with sudden snowstorms and impassable routes. Some travelers had to use ropes to lower their wagons over cliffs just to keep going.

UNFAIR TAXES

After California became a state in 1850, its government passed unfair laws against **immigrant** miners. A "foreign miner's tax" required all foreigners to pay $20 each month for the right to work in the mines. That doesn't seem like a lot of money, but it would be about $600 today. The tax targeted nonwhite miners, specifically those from China, Mexico, and South America. By 1853 the tax had been reduced to $4 a month, which would be about $120 today.

Thousands of people from China immigrated to California during the gold rush.

An International Sensation

News of California's gold rush reached beyond the United States and excited the world. California symbolized a fresh start for people struggling worldwide. Thousands of people from Asia, Europe, Australia, and South America came to California hoping to strike it rich.

The largest immigrant population came from China. Poverty, violence, and civil war had devastated the country during the 1840s. Heads of families left for California, promising to send home gold. By 1851, an estimated 25,000 Chinese were living in California.

Adventurers from Europe made the longest journey. They crossed the Atlantic then sailed around the tip of South America or crossed the Isthmus of Panama. After that, they still had to travel up the Pacific coast to California. Despite the long journey, about 30,000 Europeans came to California to mine for gold.

immigrant—a person who moves from one country to live permanently in another

Gold hunters also arrived from Australia, where failed crops sent farmers looking for new opportunities. The voyage from Australia to California took three months on the high seas.

Those who survived the journey to California had high hopes. They thought they would find a lot of gold and return home rich. But it wasn't as easy as they had hoped.

ALL ROUTES LEAD TO CALIFORNIA!

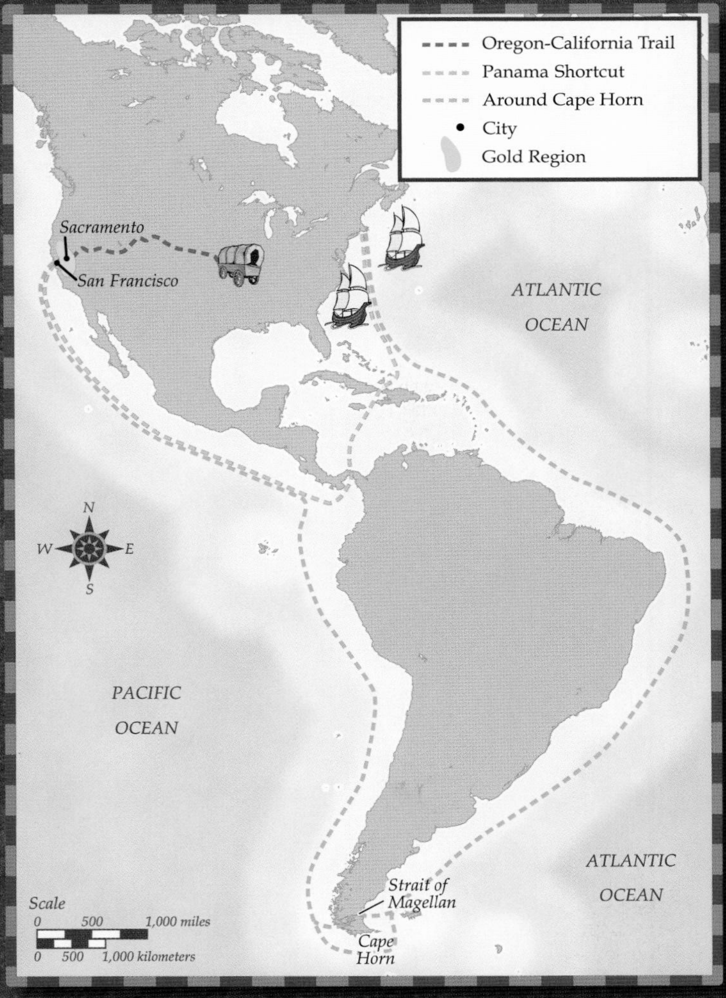

- - -	Oregon-California Trail
- - -	Panama Shortcut
- - -	Around Cape Horn
●	City
	Gold Region

Sacramento

San Francisco

ATLANTIC OCEAN

N
W   E
S

PACIFIC OCEAN

ATLANTIC OCEAN

Scale
0   500   1,000 miles
0   500   1,000 kilometers

Strait of Magellan

Cape Horn

CHAPTER 4

STAKING A CLAIM

A **pickax**, a shovel, and an iron pan—that's all a miner needed to strike it rich. Well, that and a lot of luck, because gold wasn't as plentiful as the newspapers led people to believe.

A miner pans for gold as his trusty donkeys watch.

In the beginning, many miners panned, or washed, for gold. Miners used pickaxes to break apart rocks along riverbanks and sandbars. Then they used iron pans to scoop up gravel from the river. They held the iron pans under rushing water to separate the dense gold pieces from rocks.

Miners realized they could work faster in teams. An early mining machine called a cradle needed two to four people. The first miner heaved a pickax above his head then smashed it into the riverbank. The second miner lifted the broken rock pieces into the cradle with a shovel. The third miner poured water over the cradle while the fourth miner rocked the cradle back and forth to sift out rocks and sand. It was sweaty, backbreaking labor.

Sluices, or Long Toms, were more efficient. A sluice looked like a water slide with screens. It used gravity to separate gold nuggets from ordinary rocks. Gold is denser than an ordinary rock, so it settled into grooves on the bottom of the sluice. Rushing water washed sand and rocks down the channels of the sluice, leaving any gold pieces behind.

Miners used sluices to separate gold from rocks.

pickax—a tool with a long handle and a metal head; one end of the head has a sharp blade, the other has a pick
sluice—a long slanted trough used to mine gold

Gold Rush Economics

When new miners arrived in California, their first stop was the general store to pick up supplies. Prices were high, but who cared? Everyone was absolutely certain they would find so much gold that the high prices wouldn't matter.

Merchants like Sam Brannan realized that miners needed tools, food, blankets, and clothes. Supplies were low, because getting items to California took months. The demand for shovels was especially high. Brannan sold shovels that typically cost only 20 cents for up to $50, which would equal about $1,500 today. By selling shovels and other goods, Brannan was raking in nearly $150,000 per month! That would equal about $4.5 million today! Not surprisingly, he became the first millionaire of the gold rush.

Item	Approximate U.S. Prices During Gold Rush	Approximate California Prices During Gold Rush
Blanket	$1	$12–$15
Boots	$2.50	$35
Butter	$0.15–$0.20/pound	$20/pound
Eggs	$0.03 apiece	$1–$3 apiece
Shovel	$0.25–$1.50	$15–50

Female 49ers

During the California gold rush, women made a lot of money but not usually in the mines. They cooked, washed laundry, sewed clothes, and operated hotels and restaurants. Men who mined from sunup to sundown were willing to pay almost anything for these skills. Some women made as much as $100 per week ($3,000 in modern money) washing clothes.

During the gold rush, some women made a lot of money by starting laundry businesses.

Luzena Wilson traveled from Missouri with her husband during the California gold rush. While he panned for gold, she started her own restaurant and hotel. Soon the hotel was doing so well that her husband gave up gold mining and went to work with her.

"With my own hands I chopped stakes, drove them into the ground, and set up my table. I bought provisions at a neighboring store, and when my husband came back at night he found ... 20 miners eating at my table. Each man ... put a dollar in my hand and said I might count him as a permanent customer. I called my hotel 'El Dorado.'"

—Luzena Wilson

A MINER'S LIFE

Makeshift mining camps popped up in California's river valleys. Nearly all of the inhabitants were miners who slept in cots or on the ground. It was common for a miner to have only one pair of trousers and one shirt. At first, no one bothered to dig toilets, which caused the drinking water to become contaminated. As a result, cholera killed hundreds of men. Not surprisingly, things got pretty stinky.

The miners played hard at night, dancing and gambling the time away.

> *"There is a good deal of sin and wickedness going on here. Stealing, lying, swearing, drinking, gambling, and murdering."*
>
> —Sheldon Shufelt, in an 1850 letter to his cousin

Food was expensive because the camps did not receive supplies very often. A typical miner's supper consisted of beans, biscuits, and preserved meat, like beef jerky. The unbalanced diet without fruits and vegetables caused many men to die from **scurvy**.

Mining was backbreaking work, and the gold seekers worked hard at it all day. But many miners threw away their earnings in the lawless mining camps. There, saloons and gambling tables operated around the clock. Men could lose or gain fortunes in a single game. The combination of alcohol and losing money led to fistfights and sometimes even murder.

scurvy—a deadly disease caused by lack of vitamin C; scurvy produces swollen limbs, bleeding gums, and weakness

THOMPKIN'S FERRY MASSACRE

American Indians did not like gold seekers invading their land and killing the game they needed for food. In the summer of 1851, a band of warriors traveled to a mining camp in northern California, near Thompkin's Ferry. They killed most of the miners in their sleep after slashing their tents open with tomahawks. In the following days, the surviving miners and townspeople attacked the American Indians in revenge. Miner Walter Van Dyke later wrote that "Indian villages, from Thompkin's Ferry to the mouth of the Trinity [River], were pretty much all wiped out, and many Indians belonging to them killed."

23

During the gold rush, new towns popped up wherever miners found gold. Towns like this one became ghost towns when the gold ran out.

Boom to Bust

The largest and most successful mining camps became towns where shops, restaurants, and saloons replaced canvas tents. In 1848, Sonora started out as a Mexican mining camp. By the end of 1849, the town's population had ballooned to 14,000.

In Sonora, saloons and gambling halls were decorated with crystal chandeliers. Miners could watch piano players, dancers, singers, and even circus performers for entertainment. But Sonora also had a dark side. It averaged one murder every week.

In March 1850, Dr. Thaddeus Hildreth found 30 pounds (13.6 kilograms)—nearly $5,000 worth—of gold in just two days! The exciting news spread quickly. As miners rushed to the spot, the town of Columbia appeared almost overnight. Its population skyrocketed to 5,000 in a month!

During the gold rush, miners often picked up and left one place when rumors spread that someone had struck it rich elsewhere. Therefore, when gold mining dried up in Columbia, so did the town. By 1867 it was nearly deserted. Store owners and innkeepers boarded up shop windows and moved on to seek their fortunes in other mining towns. Fancy theaters and dance halls sat empty.

In 1945 the ghost town of Columbia became a state park. Visitors to the park can get a taste of what life was like during the gold rush.

MINER LINGO

The following phrases are well known today, but they were popularized during the California gold rush.

"EUREKA!"—an exclamation of delight upon discovering gold. The word means "I have found it" in Greek.

"STRIKE IT RICH!"—to become suddenly rich! Miners who found large amounts of gold at once were said to strike it rich.

"FLASH IN THE PAN"—the excitement caused by the sight of possible gold, followed by disappointment when the "flash" was only fool's gold.

"PAYDIRT"—land that proves profitable to a miner; land that was rich with gold

"PAN OUT"—to succeed; this term comes from a popular method of mining known as panning for gold. If a miner's pan had gold in it, his claim was successful, or it had panned out.

CHAPTER 6

BIG MINING COMPANIES TAKE OVER

In 1848 and 1849, nearly every miner worked for himself. He could mine wherever he chose with the supplies he carried on his back. But by 1850, gold was becoming harder to find. Miners stopped looking for gold in rivers and turned to more expensive—and dangerous—methods.

Underground mining required a lot of money and planning. Mining companies hired teams of men to blast into mountains with dynamite. Then men with pickaxes tore open deep shafts. Some of the tunnels went down hundreds of feet beneath the earth.

Mining became dangerous work when men had to dig tunnels underground in search of gold.

Once inside the shafts, large pieces of quartz were removed using networks of buckets or small railcars. Gold sits inside the harder quartz, much like a yoke hides inside an egg. After the rocks were broken, a toxic chemical called mercury was used to separate the gold from the quartz. Many miners died from mercury poisoning, flooding, rock slides, explosive blasts, and tunnel collapses.

"Some get one, two, or even five hundred dollars some days. But half an ounce—about eight dollars—is the average. You see from this how grossly things have been misrepresented."

—Miner Hiram Pierce in a letter to his wife

Hydraulic Mining

Hydraulic mining was another method used to find gold. This method used water cannons to slowly break apart hillsides. Hydraulic mining could uncover large deposits of gold quickly, but it hurt the environment. Rocky, watery runoff destroyed rich farmland and caused flooding and **erosion**. In 1884 a judge outlawed dumping the residue created from hydraulic mining. Finally in the 1890s, hydraulic mining ceased.

Gold production peaked in 1852 when miners removed $80 million (about $2.4 billion today) worth of gold from the earth. But by then, only a few individuals got rich while the majority of men received hourly wages from large mining companies.

hydraulic—having to do with a system powered by fluid forced through pipes or chambers
erosion—the wearing away of land by water or wind

> "By this sudden discovery of the gold, all my great plans were destroyed ... Instead of being rich, I am ruined."
>
> —John Sutter

Gold and Glory

Most miners didn't keep journals, so historians are unsure how many miners made money and how many lost everything. They do know that only a few miners became rich during the California gold rush. In fact, most miners would have made more money staying at home. Even John Sutter lost his cattle, farmland, and mills when miners swarmed his property after the gold rush began.

After the gold rush started to die out around 1855, miners scattered in all directions. Some returned home, some traveled to other states to mine. Most 49ers stayed in California to start new lives. Merchants like Sam Brannan and innovators like Levi Strauss were the ones who really struck it rich.

TIMELINE

January 24, 1848
John Marshall discovers gold at Sutter's Mill.

February 2, 1848
The United States acquires land from Mexico, including California.

1849
Nearly 100,000 people travel to California to mine gold.

1852
Gold mining peaks in California.

1848   1849   1850   1851   1852

May 1848
In San Francisco, Sam Brannan announces the discovery of gold at Sutter's Mill.

December 5, 1848
President James K. Polk tells Congress about the gold discovery in California.

September 9, 1850
California becomes the 31st state of the United States.

Even so, the California gold rush forever changed the American West and the United States. Although Sutter's Fort was deserted by the 1850s, the bustling capital city of Sacramento developed around it. San Francisco kept on thriving after the gold rush, as busy merchants continued to buy, sell, and trade within the rapidly growing city.

When California became a state in 1850, the nation truly stretched from sea to shining sea. The gold rush promised endless riches. Its only guarantee was the adventure of a lifetime.

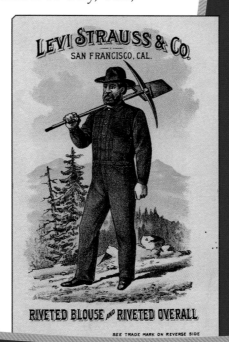

LEVI STRAUSS & CO.
SAN FRANCISCO, CAL.

RIVETED BLOUSE AND RIVETED OVERALL

SEE TRADE MARK ON REVERSE SIDE

LEVI STRAUSS

Levi Strauss moved to San Francisco in 1853. He started a company that sold dry goods, such as clothing, to small stores that then sold them to miners. He also sold denim fabric, which was used to make pants for miners and laborers.

In 1873 tailor Jacob Davis began adding metal rivets to reinforce the denim he was using to make work pants. This made the pants the sturdiest around. Davis asked Strauss to help him patent the idea, and blue jeans were born.

By the time of his death in 1902, Levi Strauss was a millionaire.

1858
The California gold rush officially ends when the discovery of pure silver in Nevada draws miners there.

1853   1854   1855   1856   1857   1858

1853
Hydraulic mining is invented.

GLOSSARY

cholera (KAH-luhr-uh)—a dangerous disease that causes severe sickness and diarrhea; cholera is caused by contaminated food or water

erosion (i-ROH-zhuhn)—the wearing away of land by water or wind

hydraulic (hye-DRAW-lik)—having to do with a system powered by fluid forced through pipes or chambers

immigrant (IM-uh-gruhnt)—a person who moves from one country to live permanently in another

isthmus (ISS-muhss)—a narrow strip of land that has water on both sides and connects two larger sections of land

malaria (muh-LAIR-ee-ah)—a serious disease that people get from mosquito bites; malaria causes high fever, chills, and sometimes death

pickax (PIK-aks)—a tool with a long handle and a metal head; one end of the head has a sharp blade, the other has a pick

pneumonia (noo-MOH-nyuh)—a serious disease that causes the lungs to become inflamed and filled with a thick fluid that makes breathing difficult

scurvy (SKUR-vee)—a deadly disease caused by lack of vitamin C; scurvy produces swollen limbs, bleeding gums, and weakness

sluice (SLOOSS)—a long slanted trough used to mine gold

yellow fever (YEL-oh FEE-vur)—an illness that can cause high fever, chills, nausea, and kidney and liver failure; liver failure causes the skin to become yellow, giving the disease its name

READ MORE

Benoit, Peter. *The California Gold Rush.* Cornerstones of Freedom. New York: Children's Press, 2013.

Collins, Terry. *Stake a Claim!: Nickolas Flux and the California Gold Rush.* Graphic Library. North Mankato, Minn.: Capstone Press, 2014.

Fradin, Dennis B. *The California Gold Rush.* Turning Points in U.S. History. New York: Marshall Cavendish Benchmark, 2009.

Landau, Elaine. *The California Gold Rush: Would You Go for the Gold?* What Would You Do? Berkeley Heights, N.J.: Enslow Publishers, 2009.

INTERNET SITES

FactHound offers a safe, fun way to find Internet sites related to this book. All of the sites on FactHound have been researched by our staff.

Here's all you do:

Visit *www.facthound.com*

Type in this code: 9781491401842

 Check out projects, games and lots more at **www.capstonekids.com**

CRITICAL THINKING USING THE COMMON CORE

1. Hundreds of thousands of people moved to California in 1849 and 1850. Name a few reasons why people headed to California hoping to "strike it rich." (Key Ideas and Details)

2. Take a look at the photograph of a sluice on page 19. How does the image help you understand how a sluice works? (Integration of Knowledge and Ideas)

3. Would you want to be a gold miner during the gold rush? Why or why not? (Text Types and Purposes)

INDEX